THIS JOURNAL BELONGS TO:

_____

Print Name

This journal is a token of love from me to you! This journal is to help you on your journey of "Self Care"

Lady Par

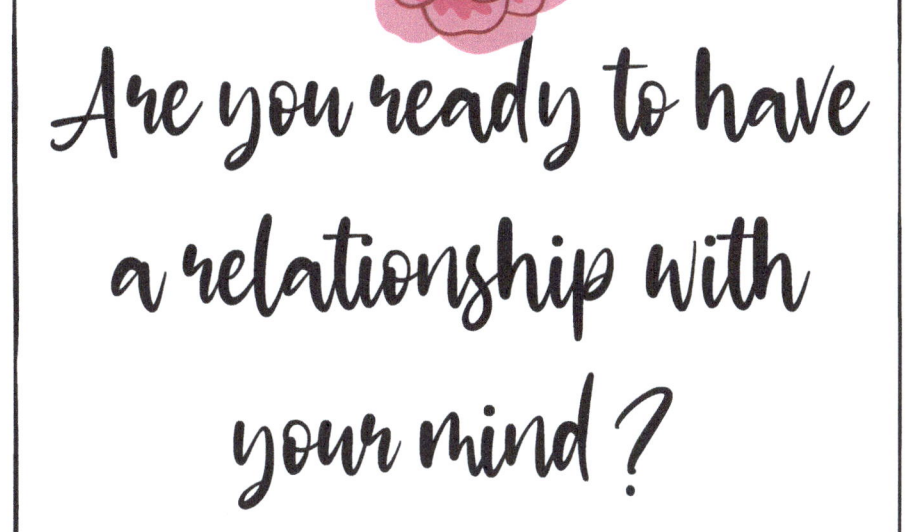

Are you ready to have a relationship with your mind?

Here is your place to release your emotions....

Journaling should be a habit to include in your everyday life. Journaling helped me narrow in on who I was & who I wanted to become. Journaling help me identify road blocks and it helped me to take the necessary steps in taking control of my life. So utilize this self-care & gratitude journal to help you on your journey of self-care.

I will succeed because I have what it takes to Walk In Them Shoes

_____

Signature required

AM Affirmation

> I am excited for what the future holds.

Date: _____

Morning

My self-care duty for today:

_____
_____
_____

Today's tasks:

_____
_____
_____

What are you thankful for today?

_____
_____

Evening

How was your day?

_____
_____
_____

Plans for tomorrow:

_____
_____
_____

P.M Affirmation

" I trust my JOURNEY "

Notes

I Got This....

AM Affirmation

" I'm deserving a beautiful day. "

Date: _____

Morning

My self-care duty for today:

_____
_____
_____

Today's tasks:

_____
_____
_____

What are you thankful for today?

_____
_____

Evening

How was your day?

_____
_____
_____

Plans for tomorrow:

_____
_____
_____

PM Affirmation

> **I AM MY RESCUE**

Notes

I Got This....

AM Affirmation

> I am proud of myself and my accomplishments

Date: _____

Morning

My self-care duty for today:

_____
_____
_____

Today's tasks:

_____
_____
_____

What are you thankful for today?

_____
_____

Evening

How was your day?

_____
_____
_____

Plans for tomorrow:

_____
_____
_____

PM Affirmation

> I turn my failures into stepping stones

Notes

I Got This....

AM Affirmation

> I LOVE &
> I ACCEPT myself
> exactly how I AM
> today.

Date: _____

Morning

My self-care duty for today:

_____
_____
_____

Today's tasks:

_____
_____
_____

What are you thankful for today?

_____
_____

Evening

How was your day?

_____
_____
_____

Plans for tomorrow:

_____
_____
_____

PM Affirmation

> I will honor my DREAMS

Notes

I Got This....

AM Affirmation

"
I embody CONFIDENCE
"

Date: _____

Morning

My self-care duty for today:

_____
_____
_____

Today's tasks:

_____
_____
_____

What are you thankful for today?

_____
_____

Evening

How was your day?

_____
_____
_____

Plans for tomorrow:

_____
_____
_____

PM
Affirmation

"

I AM
Strong & Independent

"

Notes

I Got This....

AM Affirmation

> I AM
> the creator of
> my best
> REALITY

Date: _____

Morning

My self-care duty for today:

_____
_____
_____

Today's tasks:

_____
_____
_____

What are you thankful for today?

_____
_____

Evening

How was your day?

_____
_____
_____

Plans for tomorrow:

_____
_____
_____

PM Affirmation

> My personality is amazingly off the charts!

Notes

I Got This....

AM Affirmation

"I Am Enough"

Date: _____

Morning

My self-care duty for today:

_____
_____
_____

Today's tasks:

_____
_____
_____

What are you thankful for today?

_____
_____

Evening

How was your day?

_____
_____
_____

Plans for tomorrow:

_____
_____
_____

PM Affirmation

" **I LOVE myself UNCONDITIONALLY** "

Notes

I Got This....

AM Affirmation

"**I AM Blessed**"

Date: _____

Morning

My self-care duty for today:

_____
_____
_____

Today's tasks:

_____
_____
_____

What are you thankful for today?

_____
_____

Evening

How was your day?

_____
_____

Plans for tomorrow:

_____
_____
_____

PM
Affirmation

"My _____ make me look & feel SEXY!"

Notes

I Got This....

AM Affirmation

> Money flows to me and through me.

Date: _____

Morning

My self-care duty for today:

_____
_____
_____

Today's tasks:

_____
_____
_____

What are you thankful for today?

_____
_____

Evening

How was your day?

_____
_____
_____

Plans for tomorrow:

_____
_____
_____

PM Affirmation

> "I AM driven by passion to fulfil my PURPOSE"

Notes

I Got This....

AM Affirmation

> I feel healthy and strong today!

Date: _____

Morning

My self-care duty for today:

_____
_____
_____

Today's tasks:

_____
_____
_____

What are you thankful for today?

_____
_____

Evening

How was your day?

_____
_____
_____

Plans for tomorrow:

_____
_____
_____

P.M
Affirmation

" **I AM Powerful** "

Notes

I Got This....

AM Affirmation

> "I Am Beautiful"

Date: _____

Morning

My self-care duty for today:

_____
_____
_____

Today's tasks:

_____
_____
_____

What are you thankful for today?

_____
_____

Evening

How was your day?

_____
_____
_____

Plans for tomorrow:

_____
_____
_____

PM Affirmation

"

I AM
HONEST

"

Notes

I Got This....

AM Affirmation

> I am filled with GRATITUDE today!

Date: _____

Morning

My self-care duty for today:

_____
_____
_____

Today's tasks:

_____
_____
_____

What are you thankful for today?

_____
_____

Evening

How was your day?

_____
_____
_____

Plans for tomorrow:

_____
_____
_____

PM Affirmation

> I have a voice worth hearing

Notes

I Got This....

AM Affirmation

> I AM manifesting my desires.

Date: _____

Morning

My self-care duty for today:

_____
_____
_____

Today's tasks:

_____
_____
_____

What are you thankful for today?

_____
_____

Evening

How was your day?

_____
_____

Plans for tomorrow:

_____
_____

PM Affirmation

> I am grateful for what I have.

Notes

I Got This....

AM Affirmation

> "I have all
> I need to make
> today
> **GREAT**"

Date: _____

Morning

My self-care duty for today:

_____
_____
_____

Today's tasks:

_____
_____
_____

What are you thankful for today?

_____
_____

Evening

How was your day?

_____
_____
_____

Plans for tomorrow:

_____
_____
_____

PM Affirmation

> I will PROSPER & SUCCEED

Notes

I Got This....

AM Affirmation

> I AM SUCCESSFUL

Date: _____

Morning

My self-care duty for today:

_____
_____
_____

Today's tasks:

_____
_____
_____

What are you thankful for today?

_____
_____

Evening

How was your day?

_____
_____
_____

Plans for tomorrow:

_____
_____
_____

PM Affirmation

> I am improving myself & getting closer to my goals

Notes

I Got This....

AM Affirmation

" **I AM HAPPY** "

Date: _____

Morning

My self-care duty for today:

_____
_____
_____

Today's tasks:

_____
_____
_____

What are you thankful for today?

_____
_____

Evening

How was your day?

_____
_____

Plans for tomorrow:

_____
_____
_____

PM Affirmation

> Tomorrow will be an even better day!

Notes

I Got This....

AM Affirmation

> **I AM creating the life I WANT**

Date: _____

Morning

My self-care duty for today:
_____
_____
_____

Today's tasks:
_____
_____
_____

What are you thankful for today?
_____
_____

Evening

How was your day?
_____
_____
_____

Plans for tomorrow:
_____
_____
_____

PM Affirmation

"

I AM
in charge of how
I Feel

"

Notes

I Got This....

AM Affirmation

> **I AM COURAGEOUS & CONFIDENT**

Date: _____

Morning

My self-care duty for today:

_____
_____
_____

Today's tasks:

_____
_____
_____

What are you thankful for today?

_____
_____

Evening

How was your day?

_____
_____
_____

Plans for tomorrow:

_____
_____
_____

PM Affirmation

> Even though I have messed up in the past, I can still create a positive future!

Notes

I Got This....

AM Affirmation

> "I have the knowledge to make smart decisions for myself today."

Date: _____

Morning

My self-care duty for today:

_____
_____
_____

Today's tasks:

_____
_____
_____

What are you thankful for today?

_____
_____

Evening

How was your day?

_____
_____
_____

Plans for tomorrow:

_____
_____
_____

P.M Affirmation

"**I AM Healed of—**"

Notes

I Got This....

AM Affirmation

> "I am patient and calm"

Date: _____

Morning

My self-care duty for today:

_____
_____
_____

Today's tasks:

_____
_____
_____

What are you thankful for today?

_____
_____

Evening

How was your day?

_____
_____
_____

Plans for tomorrow:

_____
_____
_____

PM Affirmation

"
I AM
my
RESCUE
"

Notes

I Got This....

AM Affirmation

> I AM LOVE.
> I AM LOVE.
> I AM LOVE.

Date: _____

Morning

My self-care duty for today:

_____
_____
_____

Today's tasks:

_____
_____
_____

What are you thankful for today?

_____
_____

Evening

How was your day?

_____
_____
_____

Plans for tomorrow:

_____
_____
_____

PM Affirmation

> "I make good **CHOICES**"

Notes

I Got This....

Notes

I Got This....

Notes

I Got This....

Notes

I Got This....

Notes

I Got This....

Notes

I Got This....

Notes

I Got This....

Notes

I Got This....

Notes

I Got This....

Notes

I Got This....

Notes

I Got This....

Notes

I Got This....

Made in the USA
Columbia, SC
17 August 2022